HANDBOOK

MW00366615

SOUL

Christianity
EXPLORED

Soul Handbook (3rd Edition)
Copyright © 2013 Christianity Explored

www.ceministries.org

Published by
The Good Book Company Ltd
Tel: 0333 123 0880; International: +44 (0) 208 942 0880
Email: admin@thegoodbook.co.uk

Websites:
UK: www.thegoodbook.co.uk
North America: www.thegoodbook.com
Australia: www.thegoodbook.com.au
New Zealand: www.thegoodbook.co.nz

CHRISTIANITY
E✝PLORED
MINISTRIES

Unless otherwise indicated, Scripture is taken from the HOLY BIBLE, NEW INTERNATIONAL
VERSION. Copyright © 1973, 1978, 1984 International Bible Society.

Used by permission of Zondervan Bible Publishers.

All rights reserved. Except as may be permitted by the Copyright Act, no portion of this publication
may be reproduced in any form or by any means without prior permission from the publisher.

ISBN: 9781908762696

Design by Steve Devane and André Parker

Printed in China

SOUL

1 Christianity is Christ

▶ If you could ask God one question, and you knew it would be answered, what would it be?

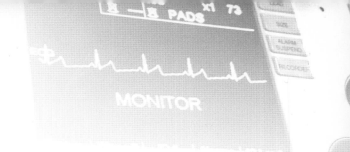

READ MARK 1:1

▶ What does Mark say Christianity is all about in the first sentence of his book?

▶ How is that different from some of the pictures we've drawn?

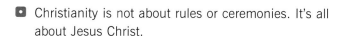

- Christianity is not about rules or ceremonies. It's all about Jesus Christ.

- If we're here by chance, we have no real significance or value. But God created us – so we matter enormously.

- We all face death sooner or later. Since we all have to die, what's the point of living?

- The Bible says we don't really start living until we know the one who made us, and live as he made us to live.

- But how can we get to know God? We need him to reveal himself to us. Mark says he's done that for us by sending Jesus Christ. If we want to know what God is like, we must look at Jesus.

- That's why "the gospel about Jesus Christ" is good news.

▶ If you asked a group of people in the street: "What's the point of life?", what kind of answers would you get?

▶ What do most people think about God and Christianity? Why do you think that is?

▶ What about Jesus?
Do people think he matters? What do *you* think?

2 Identity

▶ Think of your best friend. What do you really like about them?

READ MARK 2:1–12

▶ Why is the house full at the start of this passage? (Look at Mark 1:45 for clues.)

> Imagine you were in the room. How would you have reacted to Jesus saying: *"Son, your sins are forgiven"?* (See verse 5.) Why do you think he said it?

> Why do the religious leaders react so strongly when Jesus forgives the man's sin? (See verse 7.)
Do you think their response is right?

> Jesus heals the man so that he can walk. What's the real reason Jesus healed him? (Look at verse 10 for a clue.)

download

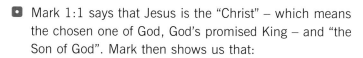

- Mark 1:1 says that Jesus is the "Christ" – which means the chosen one of God, God's promised King – and "the Son of God". Mark then shows us that:

- Jesus can forgive sins – **Mark 2:1–10**

- Jesus has power to heal – **Mark 2:11–12**

- Jesus has power over nature – **Mark 4:35–41**

- Jesus has power over demons – **Mark 5:1–17**

- Jesus has power over death – **Mark 5:35–42**

❯ Which of the events Mark tells us about would you have found most amazing or scary?
Why?

❯ What do *you* think of Jesus?

3 Mission

❯ What do you think is the biggest problem facing the world?

❯ From last time's *Soul*, what does Jesus think is the biggest problem facing the world?

▶ What does it mean to love God with all your heart, with all your soul, with all your mind and with all your strength?

▶ What does it mean to love your neighbour as yourself?

▶ How good do you think you are at living up to these two commands? Where do you especially fall down?

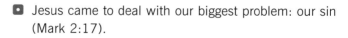

- Jesus came to deal with our biggest problem: our sin (Mark 2:17).

- Each and every one of us rebels against our loving Creator. That rebellion is what the Bible calls "sin".

- Sin is a serious problem that will lead us to hell. If we continue to reject God, then he will respond to that decision – and reject us.

- Only Jesus can rescue us from the problem of sin. Jesus came to rescue rebels.

▶ What are some of the reasons people give for why Jesus came?

▶ Do you think sin is a problem? Why or why not?

▶ How would you feel if all your thoughts, words and actions were on display for everyone to see?

4 Cross

▶ Imagine you know how and when you will die. How would it make you feel?

▶ What would it lead you to do?

▶ What does Peter realize in verse 29?

▶ Why would Jesus' words in verse 31 surprise Peter?

▶ Why does Jesus confront Peter in verse 33?

▶ When Jesus died on the cross, was it unexpected?
(Look at Mark 9:31 and Mark 10:33–34 for clues.)

download

- Jesus knew when he was going to die. His death wasn't an accident – it was planned.

- Jesus' death is the only way we can be saved from our sin. It is the way Jesus rescues us, as "a ransom for many" (Mark 10:45).

- When Jesus died, he was willingly taking the punishment for *our* sin. He was punished in *our* place, so that *we* can be rescued.

- Jesus' death makes it possible for us to be accepted by God and enjoy a relationship with him.

- People have different reactions to Jesus' death: Pontius Pilate goes with the crowd; the soldiers are wrapped up in themselves; the religious leaders think they don't need Jesus; the Roman centurion gets it right, when he says that Jesus is "the Son of God".

▶ How would you feel if someone else deliberately took the punishment for something serious you had done wrong?

▶ Why do you think Jesus' death on the cross is so important to Christians?

▶ Which of the reactions to Jesus' death is most like your reaction?

5 Resurrection

▶ What would be your first reaction if you heard that someone had come back from the dead?

READ MARK 15:42 – 16:8

▶ Why are the women worried as they approach the tomb? (See Mark 16:3.)

> Find four things that surprise them when they arrive.
(See verses 4–6.)

> Should they have been surprised that Jesus rose from the
dead? (Look at Mark 8:31, 9:30–31, 10:32–34 for clues.)

> Why do you think the women ran away from the tomb?

download

- If Jesus has not risen from the dead, Christianity collapses.

- The resurrection proves that Jesus is who he says he is, and that his death was a ransom for many.

- Jesus did die: Pontius Pilate, the Roman centurion, Joseph of Arimathea and the women were all certain that Jesus had died.

- Jesus did rise: the tomb was empty; Jesus was seen alive by hundreds of people, many of whom were later killed for insisting that he was alive.

- The resurrection proves that Jesus will come again as Judge of the whole world (Acts 17:31).

- The resurrection means that death has been defeated. If we trust in Jesus, we can have confidence that God will raise us from death.

▶ What part of the evidence for Jesus' resurrection do you find most convincing? Why?

▶ Do you think that Jesus rose from the dead?
Why or why not?

▶ Why does Jesus' resurrection matter, if at all?

6 Grace

▸ What things do people do so others will accept them?

▸ What things do people do to be accepted by God?

▶ Why does the man think God should accept him?

▶ What is Jesus' response?

▶ Why does the man leave? What does that show about the man?

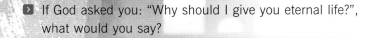

> If God asked you: "Why should I give you eternal life?",
> what would you say?

■ Most people think God will accept them because of
things they have done or haven't done. But these things
can't solve the problem of sin.

■ The Bible tells us that God accepts us, not because of
anything *we've* done, but because of what *Jesus* has
done.

■ Like the man with the skin disease, we need to ask
Jesus to make us clean (Mark 1:40-42).

■ The only way we can be accepted by God is because he
sent Jesus to die on the cross in our place.

■ Grace is God's undeserved gift to us. Because of what
Jesus has done, God treats us in a way we don't
deserve.

❯ What exactly is grace?
How would you explain it if someone asked you?

❯ What do people find offensive about grace?
What does it say about us?

❯ What is so wonderful about grace? What does it offer us?

❯ What does grace tell us about the character of God?

The Holy Spirit

- The Holy Spirit, who comes to live in Christians, is the Spirit of Jesus himself – the Holy Spirit is God.

- The Holy Spirit has a number of roles including:
  - guiding followers of Jesus
  - showing people their sin
  - changing people by giving them the desire to please God.

- Jesus promises that when we trust in him, he will come and live in us forever by his Spirit (John 14:15-17).

▶ Before *Soul*, what did you know about the Holy Spirit?

▶ What did you find most surprising about who the Holy Spirit is or what the Holy Spirit does?

▶ How do you feel about the Spirit of Jesus coming to live "with you" and "in you" (John 14:17)?

Church

- In the Bible, "the church" is not a building – it's a group of Christians who follow Christ together.

- The Holy Spirit unites Christians as members of God's family.

- If we're to live the Christian life, we need to help each other.

- A good church is where Christians listen carefully to God's word – the Bible – and change how they think and live as a result. They also encourage each other, remember Jesus' death and resurrection, and pray together.

▶ What has been your experience of church?
Was it positive or negative?

▶ What do you think God's family *should* be like?

▶ What difference do you think a good church should make to
someone who's trying to follow Jesus?

Talk

download

inside track

- The Bible and prayer are vital to the Christian life. When we read the Bible, God talks to us. When we pray, we talk to God.

- The Bible enables us to be strong and to keep going in the Christian life.

- Christians can pray to God about anything, knowing that he is in control of everything.

❯ Have you read any parts of the Bible?
What did you like about them?
What did you find difficult?

❯ Do you ever pray?
What kind of things do you say to God?
When are you most likely to talk to God?

❯ What do you think you might find most difficult about praying and reading the Bible?

7 So what?

▶ We started *Soul* by asking: "If you could ask God one question, what would it be?"

▶ If God were to ask *you* one question, what do you think it would be?

READ MARK 1:14–15

▶ What do you think Jesus means by "the good news of God"?

▶ What does Jesus mean when he says: "The time has come" and "The kingdom of God is near"?

▶ What do you think the word "repent" means?

▶ What do you think it means to "believe the good news"?

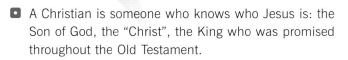

- A Christian is someone who knows who Jesus is: the Son of God, the "Christ", the King who was promised throughout the Old Testament.

- A Christian is someone who understands why Jesus came: he came to die as the only way sinful people can be brought back into a relationship with God.

- A Christian is someone who follows Jesus:
  Jesus says: "If anyone would come after me, he must deny himself and take up his cross and follow me" (Mark 8:34). Denying self means no longer living for ourselves but for Jesus and others. Taking up our cross means being prepared to follow him, whatever the cost.

- Jesus gives a convincing reason to live like this: "Whoever loses his life for me and for the gospel will save it" (Mark 8:35). If we give our lives to him, he will save them. We will know and enjoy God now, and spend eternity with him when we die.

▶ How would you score the following statements?
   (0 = completely unconvinced; 10 = very sure)

- ◉ Jesus is God.

- ◉ Jesus came to rescue us from our sin.

- ◉ Following Jesus means denying ourselves
  and putting Jesus first, whatever the cost.

▶ What choices will you make now that you've finished *Soul*?
   What is the next step for you?

The Mark Challenge

You can read through Mark's Gospel in less than two hours. But to really think about what he is telling us about Jesus, it is better to take it slowly. Use the reading plan below to work your way through Mark, taking time to think about what you read.

- ■ **Day 1.** Mark 1:1-28
- ■ **Day 2.** Mark 1:29 – 2:12
- ■ **Day 3.** Mark 2:13 – 3:6
- ■ **Day 4.** Mark 3:7-35
- ■ **Day 5.** Mark 4:1-41
- ■ **Day 6.** Mark 5:1-20
- ■ **Day 7.** Mark 5:21-43
- ■ **Day 8.** Mark 6:1-29
- ■ **Day 9.** Mark 6:30-56
- ■ **Day 10.** Mark 7:1-37
- ■ **Day 11.** Mark 8:1-38

- ■ **Day 12.** Mark 9:1-32
- ■ **Day 13.** Mark 9:33 – 10:16
- ■ **Day 14.** Mark 10:17-52
- ■ **Day 15.** Mark 11:1-33
- ■ **Day 16.** Mark 12:1-44
- ■ **Day 17.** Mark 13:1-37
- ■ **Day 18.** Mark 14:1-52
- ■ **Day 19.** Mark 14:53 – 15:15
- ■ **Day 20.** Mark 15:16-47
- ■ **Day 21.** Mark 16:1-8

A note about chapters and verses

Throughout Mark's book you will see some large numbers and some smaller numbers. The larger numbers are the chapters Mark has been split into. The smaller numbers are the verses that make up each chapter. The chapters and verses weren't in the original but have been added later to help us find our way around. We often use a kind of shorthand so that Mark chapter 1 and verse 1 will be written as "Mark 1:1" or sometimes as "Mark 1 v 1".

■ Mark tells us about the amazing things Jesus did and said. He also tells us where Jesus was at the time. Use the map to help you follow the story as Jesus travels around the country of Israel.

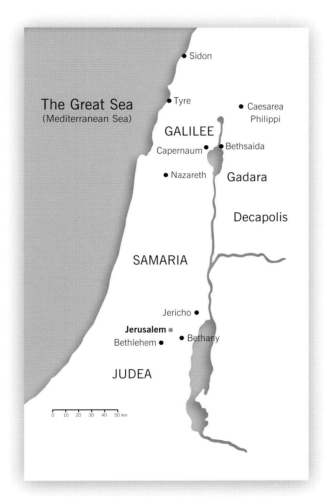